Saying the Things We Think
but Rarely Say Out Loud

BY

LA'SHONDRA JOHNSON

How to use this book

Grabs microphone like I just won an Oscar First things first...I just want to thank GOD!
(*Insert cheers and dramatic music fade-out*)

Okay, okay—on a more serious note...

Thank you for picking up this book and choosing to invest in yourself, your voice, and your growth. Whether you bought this because your relationships feel a little crunchy or because your workplace communication is giving "passive-aggressive email thread" energy—you're in the right place.

This book is meant to be a **quick, informative (and let's be honest, entertaining)** read. It's packed with stories based on real-life scenarios I've lived—or walked through with my clients—in both business *and* personal life. Of course, names and details have been changed to protect the not-so-innocent.

I want you to treat this book like a **buffet** (yes, I said it—and yes, I love food, so ride with me here). There's a lot to taste—tips, tools, tea—and it's not meant to be devoured in one sitting. Make multiple trips. Come back for seconds, thirds, or dessert later when life hands you a new communication challenge.

This book is meant to **feed you for years to come**. Let it be your go-to recipe for better conversations, stronger boundaries, and communication that actually connects.

Because let's be real: relationships rise or fall based on how we talk—and how we don't.

And here's what I've learned:
We are slowly unlearning how to be great communicators.
Text messages, social media, and ghosting culture are making us forget the value of presence, clarity, and empathy.
No matter how "good" you think you are at speaking, I promise—there's always room for growth.
And just when you think you've mastered it, life will hand you a fresh new test in the form of a client, a partner, or a conflict you didn't see coming.

So, sit back. Laugh. Reflect. Highlight like crazy.
Let the stories hit. Let the tips stick.
And most importantly—**practice what speaks to you.**

Because this book only works if *you* do.

Now, let's take it back to the beginning.
And since I'm about to get all up in **your** business—
Let me start by letting you in on a little secret of **mine**...

How it all started

I was sitting in my car, still parked outside the house. The keys were in the ignition, but I hadn't turned my car off. My hand just rested there. Phone open. Thumb hovering. I had typed the message… then deleted it. Typed it again… deleted it again. Why was this so hard? Why was I thinking so much.

It wasn't even that deep. Just a "Hey, can we talk?"

But every version of his potential reaction started playing like a trailer in my head: the sigh, the silence, the shift. The worst one? Him reading it and not responding at all (my biggest fear that I KNEW could send me spiraling).

I stared at the screen and felt that familiar heat rise up my neck — the anxious kind. Not anger. Not sadness. Just that weird ache that says: "Don't say too much. Don't mess it up."

And I hated that. I hated that speaking up felt like a risk. Like I had to rehearse being human.

Which often left me with two decisions: let him reach out first or call awkwardly and possible make things worse (since I was already nervous and overthinking, the latter idea felt inevitable).

Have you all been here before? I thought I was just an anxious communicator in romantic relationships, but when I really sat back to think about it, I've been this way in business too.

Just like in my romantic scenario, for a business decision I hovered over the "Send" button like it had the power to detonate something.

It was just a follow-up email. But in it, I had written the number I wanted.

Not the "safe" number. Not the "I hope this doesn't offend you" rate. The real one — the one I had earned.

And I swear, the second I typed it, my stomach did a backflip.

Was I asking for too much?

Would they laugh? Ghost me? Tell other people I was "difficult to work with"?

That old, tired voice came creeping in: "Just be grateful. Don't rock the boat."

But another voice — quieter, but stronger — whispered back:

"You're not rocking the boat. You're building the damn dock."

Still, my finger hovered.

Clicking "Send" felt like jumping without a net.

But I knew — if I wanted to be paid what I was worth, I had to stop negotiating against myself first.

And this is when it hit me— I wasn't just struggling in one area, I was struggling in all when it came to uncomfortable conversations with others where I had to speak up AND deal with the possibility of conflict after.

Where it all started

When I was a kid, I thought I knew everything — and I said everything.

I rarely thought before I spoke. I'd just let my mouth fly open and the words would tumble out. Shy? Never heard of her. I was loud, present, outspoken. I was theatrical, too — always dreaming up skits and acting them out with my cousins on Sundays after church.

(Anybody else grow up "creating" with their cousins?)

I didn't think there was anything wrong with how I was.
Until I became a teenager.

Suddenly, everything shifted.

I started hearing that I was "too much."
Too loud.
Too confident.
Too nice.
Too trusting.

Too EXTRA/Dramatic *rolls eyes*

People took advantage of that, and I slowly began to shrink. I just wanted to be liked. To be loved.

I wanted friends. I wanted guys to like me. I wanted my family to stop calling me dramatic every time I expressed myself.
So the question quietly entered my mind:
"What do I have to *be* in order to be accepted?"

And just like that, my people-pleasing era began.

I became whoever I thought I needed to be — in every room, for every person — just to gain approval. That included being the girl who *never* brought up when she was hurt.
Especially not to people I cared about.

I avoided conflict like it was a disease — at least with those I deemed important.
But that avoidance?
It followed me into adulthood.

I became the magnetic woman who could light up any room... but couldn't sustain real, authentic relationships for too long. Why?
Because I was performing.

Just like those skits on Sundays.

After most encounters, I'd walk away *exhausted* from trying to say the right things, avoid the landmines, and be the "perfect" conversationalist. Especially when it came to conflict in my personal life.

But here's the truth:
You can't avoid messy conversations forever.
And honestly? Some of them aren't even messy.
They're just **necessary**.

56% of people admit they've avoided a difficult conversation because of an **internal narrative** about how it would go wrong. *(Crucial Conversations /Dialogue Works)* And if you can't avoid conflict, then you try to give the perfect response.

The more I tried to be perfect in my relationships, the more I messed up — not because I was bad at relationships, but because perfection is impossible. And trying to maintain it is *draining.*

What I didn't realize was that even in business, where my polished exterior seemed to help me, I still wasn't being seen as fully authentic.
I was dodging necessary conversations.
I wasn't growing the way I needed to.

I was still stuck in the belief that if I appeared perfect, people would like me — and want to work with me.
But here's what I know now:

People liked me...
But people **loved** me more when I got *real.*

I do business better when I stop avoiding hard conversations. When I walk into rooms and conversations comfortable with myself enough to KNOW I CAN handle these conversations.

Because the conversations we avoid in our personal lives?
They show up in our business lives too.

And when I became a business coach, that truth hit even harder:
I'm not the only one.

Introduction

WHICH ONE ARE YOU?

I've spent my whole life talking. From being *voluntold* to recite scriptures at church, to joining my theater magnet program, all the way to competing—and winning—in oratory and pitch competitions. Talking is like breathing for me... or at least that's what I thought.

I've built a career teaching people how to write speeches and present themselves on stage. But through my own trial and error—and by watching my clients—I realized something important: a lot of us are **leaving way too much unsaid**, and it's hurting us more than we realize.

Most people fall into one of three categories:

1. **Strugglers in both life and business** – People who have a hard time advocating for themselves personally often struggle in business too.
2. **High-functionary in one area** – People who kill it in business but shrink in personal relationships (or vice versa). These folks are often high-functioning but performative. (*Hi, it's me.*)
3. **Balanced communicators** – People who've found their "Voice." They communicate with confidence in both personal and professional spaces. They're rare—but not mythical.

Trigger Warning Ahead (Prepare to be uncomfortable)
Most of my clients fall in category 1 or 2. But WHY?

Category 1: The Overwhelmed & Underheard

If you're struggling personally **and** professionally (category 1), chances are you're in survival mode. Your life might lack structure, routine, or clarity. That chaos bleeds into your business because your business is an extension of you. If you haven't mastered discipline over your life (not perfection—**discipline**), then building a business will feel like building on sand. Your clarity, confidence, and communication are tied to your personal foundation. You don't understand Who you are and your WHY. Why did you create this business? Why do people need to work with you? Why is this important to you and to those you think you can serve? A lot of people (especially those just starting out), are all over the place with their business ideas (this is normal, you're trying to figure out the structure), but when personal life is also chaotic, it can make your vision unclear and you have NO IDEA what you really want to say about yourself or your business.

Category 2: The Performers

These are the people doing well in one area—but that's about it.

Maybe you're a beast in business, but your personal relationships are a mess. Or maybe you're nurturing and loving at home, but feel invisible at work. You've learned to compartmentalize, but it's not sustainable.

I see this a lot with women who lead. They can give boardroom boss energy but struggle to show up authentically at home. They're not using the same communication skills across the board—and it's costing them peace and connection.

They understand discipline ENOUGH, and their niche market ENOUGH, but for some reason, the balance in their personal life is not balancing ENOUGH! These people (I typically serve women, but men take what you need here), struggle with understanding how to leave Boardroom/ Corporate Room Nancy at the office and turn into the wife/girlfriend

/mom/friend that they need to be. They are lacking balance, not communicating effectively like they do at work and often times question– why is it easier at work than it is with family/friends? Because you're lacking balance in life! It is important to be balanced in life, to be balanced in our communication patterns.

Category 3: The Balanced Ones

The rare few who fall into Category 3 have something most people don't: a clear sense of self. They've found "The Voice." It doesn't mean they're perfect, but it does mean they've developed the emotional intelligence and communication tools to navigate both boardrooms and bedrooms with confidence.

And when they slip (because we all do), they know how to find their way back.

Most people are delulu enough to think this is them (don't get offended, just wear the shoe if it's yours), but if I interviewed many peoples closest friends and families they would say "NO Darnell is completely work oriented and comes home as a tyrant" or "NO, Michelle gets quiet during conflict and shuts down, but is able to resolve work conflict easy."

Category 3 individuals once again, are NOT perfect, and sometimes, they even slip in category 1 or 2. The biggest difference between them and category 1 and 2, is they are able to balance themselves out. They don't live in the other categories, but as humans they at times slip into moments where they lose "The Voice." They always find their way back to it.

> If you haven't caught on yet, let me make it plain—**balancing your communication skills will make your life easier.**

85% of job success comes from soft skills, not hard skills (Harvard, Stanford, Carnegie Foundation). So what does that mean? Your ability to speak, connect, manage conflict, and so much more determines your success in every area of your life, both personally and business wise.

> In this book, we're going to break down what it takes to communicate with clarity and confidence across the board. You'll learn how to build a strong self-image, show up powerfully in your career, and handle even the messiest personal conversations with grace.

And we are going to discuss how you can have it all— a healthy self image (it starts there),a career where you feel confident, and personal connections that you can navigate even the toughest challenges with ease (because you understand yourself, and you understand people)!

> Because here's the truth: if you don't believe in yourself **personally**, your business persona is just a performance. And performances lead to burnout.
>
> I'm here to help you thrive by having all the conversations we *should* be having (but usually don't).We're about to get into the stuff people avoid because that's where the breakthroughs live.
>
> In this book you're going to meet some amazing people who embody actual people I've worked with, their real life scenarios, and just for a little extra realism, I've even included some of my own personal struggles that I've overcome as well. But for the purpose of this book, you will meet them through my character portrayals of Robert and Tanya, and a few of their friends along the way.
>
> Buckle up, baby. We've got messy conversations to untangle—and I'm not sparing your feelings.

Part 1

THE MESS WE MAKE—WHAT'S LEFT UNSAID CAN COST YOU!

We've all been there—staring at a text we didn't send, replaying a conversation we should've had, or wondering why someone suddenly pulled away. Sometimes, the damage in our relationships isn't caused by what we said—it's by what we didn't say.

This section is about the unspoken stuff. The silence that creates distance–and financial mayhem. The assumptions that build walls. The small moments of miscommunication that snowball into big misunderstandings.

In Part 1, we're going to unpack the everyday ways we unintentionally sabotage connections—with our partners, our friends, our families, even at work. We don't even realize we're doing it.

But here's the kicker: **our money is impacted, too.** Quiet tension around finances can bleed into overspending, unclear agreements, missed opportunities, and resentment.

For the sake of keeping it real (while protecting the privacy of those I've worked with or been in relationships with), you'll see a blend of real-life scenarios—broken down through both a personal and professional lens.

Let's get honest about the mess—so we can start learning how to clean it up.

And remember: **clear language doesn't require perfection—just intention.**

Chapter 1

THE ART OF SAYING NOTHING (AND WHY IT'S COSTING YOU)

Tanya and Robert have settled in for a quiet night at home. Things have been going well between them—on the surface. But Tanya has a few concerns about their future, especially around finances and shared planning.

She's hinted at wanting a "check-in," something she only brings up when it's time for a deeper conversation. Robert knows this pattern, and truthfully? He'd rather not go there. She only brings this up when the conversation is about something serious, and unfortunately, this conversation can easily go wrong. Robert is NOT interested in any type of disagreement. When Tanya finally brings up the real concern– saving up for their wedding and sharing more openly about their finances (or that's what he thinks he heard)-- he simply smiled, nodded, and said:

"Whatever you want, babe," Robert said quickly, not meeting her eyes.

Tanya paused. "Wait—do you actually agree, or are you just saying that to avoid a fight?"

He shrugged. "Does it matter?"

"Yes," she said. "Because I don't want a fake 'yes' that turns into real resentment."

But something in his tone didn't match the words. It wasn't agreement—it was retreat. He wasn't saying yes. He was saying, please let this end so we don't fight.

She wanted to feel excited. Instead, she felt... alone. Uncertain. And even though no one yelled, it felt like something broke right there between them.

Avoidance Costs More Than Discomfort:

Whether it's romance, business, or family—avoiding hard conversations might buy you a moment of peace, but it often costs you connection, trust, and long-term clarity.

In business, deals fall apart when people say yes just to close, but walk away with silent doubts or misaligned expectations. In any relationship, silence can become resentment.For Robert he not only avoids tough conversations in his relationshipt,he often resents where his career is or certain relationships with peers and leaders could be better, and he also often chooses to disengage when their could be a conflict. He instead will just say "Yes" as a easier solution to getting things done, despite how he feels or confusion he may have. While he feels it gets him along enough, his business career is stagnant and connections are lacking, and his own fiance finds him avoidant. And when avoidance becomes a pattern, so does disconnection.

69% of employees say they **avoid difficult conversations**, especially when emotions are high or stakes are personal (Crucial Learning, 2021) **86%** of employees and executives cite **lack of collaboration or ineffective communication** as the main reason for workplace failures (Salesforce).

Everything begins and ends with a conversation. And just like in business, relationship require negotiation and uncomfortable conversations at times to come to a compromise that works for all parties.

Statistics show that most people are not negotiating– in relationships and in business–especially when it comes to what they are bein paid upfront. And women are even less likely to negotiate than men. The question is–Why?

Tactical Analysis: Why We Avoid Negotiation–and What to Do Instead

People Fear Confrontation:

1. Fear of rejection or disappointing others

Many people avoid confrontation not because they don't have something to say—but because they fear *what the other person will think* of them if they say it.

- "Will they be mad at me?"
- "What if they pull away?"
- "What if I ruin the relationship?"

This fear is rooted in our deep need for belonging and approval. For some, speaking up feels like risking connection—and they'd rather be uncomfortable than feel unwanted.

2. Negative past experiences with conflict

If someone grew up in a household (or past workplace or relationship) where conflict was loud, violent, or emotionally unsafe, they may associate disagreement with danger.
They've learned:

> "Speaking up = getting yelled at or shut down."

So even as adults, their nervous system interprets conflict as a threat—not just a conversation. They flinch, freeze, or flee—even when the stakes aren't high.

3. Unclear communication models growing up (e.g., "Don't rock the boat" mindset)

For many people, conflict avoidance is **generational and cultural**. They were taught—explicitly or subtly—to keep the peace at all costs.

- "If you can't say something nice, don't say anything at all."
- "Let it go."
- "Children are to be seen and not heard"
- "Keep your head down."

The result? They never learned how to disagree *respectfully*, only how to suppress. So when tension arises, they either shut down or explode—because healthy in-between tools were never modeled.

4. A belief that harmony = agreement

Some people mistakenly think that the absence of conflict means everything is fine.
But real harmony doesn't come from avoiding hard conversations—it comes from *working through them with honesty and care.*
This mindset sounds like:

- "I just want everyone to get along."
- "I'd rather keep the peace than cause a scene."
  But over time, this peacekeeping leads to resentment, misunderstanding, and often, relational distance.

Business Parallel - When "Yes" Means "I'm Not Sure"

I get it — negotiating in business can feel different than negotiating in a romantic relationship... but honestly? It's really not.

Instead of *"going along to get along,"* it's time to take more control of your relationships — personal and professional.

As a small business owner, I've found myself in multiple situations where negotiation was necessary. I've been offered deals that looked great on paper... but something felt off.
Too many assumptions.
Not enough clarity.
Especially around money and expectations.
And every time I didn't ask the hard questions, didn't negotiate my worth, or didn't clarify what was expected of *me* (and what *I* expected in return), I ended up frustrated — doing way more work than the compensation covered.

Why?
Because I was scared.
Scared of coming across as "difficult."
Scared of missing an opportunity.
Scared of being told no.

But one day, I decided to stop rushing and start protecting my peace — and my business.

Now? I give myself **24–48 hours** before making any major decisions. I no longer sign under pressure.
Instead, I respond with something like:

> *"I'm really interested in working together, but before I commit, I'd like to clarify a few expectations so we're both set up for success."*

That one line has saved my energy, my integrity, and my reputation more than once.

Here's the truth:

Boundaries aren't blocks — they're bridges to better outcomes.

And an important reminder:
In business, you *have* to be okay with walking away if a deal doesn't make sense for both sides.
If you're afraid to walk away, you're operating from fear — and fear leads to burnout.

Don't hold on to potential business so tightly that you forget your own value.

Every partnership should be mutually beneficial.
And if someone isn't willing to treat you — and your work — with the respect it deserves?

Be willing to *walk.*

> *Pause here. Think of a time you nodded yes but didn't mean it. What did it feel like?*

What to Do Instead:

1. Identify the potential conflict as is(don't add any emotion)
    a. Whether it's financial issues, cheating,etc. Identify the conflict without the emotion. Focus on the facts first and why it needs to be addressed.
2. Name the Emotion you are feeling due to this conflict (Without Blame)
    b. Say: "I'm feeling unsure about this and I want to be honest with you."
    c. Don't say: "You're pressuring me."
3. Create Safe Check-In Moments
    d. In business or love, ask: "Can we pause and make sure we're on the same page?"

4. Reframe Conflict as Clarity
   e. You're not fighting. You're aligning. The most solid connections are built through honest, not easy, conversations.

Bottom Line:

Keeping the peace externally while chaos builds internally is a recipe for relational burnout. Let this chapter be your invitation to say the thing—with care, not combat. Because peace built on silence doesn't last (trust me, I have tried!)

Let's go back to Tanya and her fiance. Same table, same topic. But this time, instead of shrinking into silence, he takes a breath and says:

"Okay. Can I be honest with you first?"

Tanya nodded, surprised.

"I really want to plan our future together. And I've also realized I get nervous when we talk about finances—I don't always know the 'right' answer, and sometimes I shut down because I don't want to disappoint you or say the wrong thing."

Tanya's expression softened. "Thank you for saying that," she said. "I don't need you to have all the answers. I just want us to have a space where we can talk about it—even if it's uncomfortable."

Robert exhaled. "That helps a lot. I want us to be a team. Can we figure this out together—maybe start by just talking about our expectations? Like what we both hope for financially before the wedding and even what a shared system could look like?"

Tanya smiled, relieved. "That's exactly what I want too. Let's talk it through—step by step."

And for the first time in a while, they didn't walk away from the table feeling misunderstood. They didn't land on every detail perfectly—but they landed on each other, and that was enough

> "I really care about this relationship, and I want us to move forward. But I have some worries about how we'd handle finances, and I think we should talk about it openly."

There's a pause. Not tense—*honest.* Tanya leans in, not away. And just like that, their relationship deepens—not because they agreed, but because they were willing to *understand.*

Will it be perfect all the time?NO. Can it become messy?YES. But you are not doing anyone any favors by being silent or just saying yes. Embrace the discomfort that comes with establishing your voice and your boundaries in every area of life. The more you lean in, the more comfortable you will get over time.

Journal Prompt

When have I agreed to something just to keep the peace?

What did it cost me in clarity, energy, or trust?

What could I say differently next time to honor myself and the relationship?

Chapter 2

MONEY, EMOTIONS, AND MESSY TRUTHS

The Conversations We Delay Until It's Too Late

In Chapter 1, we met Tanya—a more balanced communicator—and Robert, who shifts between being a *Performer* and, at times, someone who feels overwhelmed and underheard.

It's important to remember that different scenarios can bring out different sides of our communication style—especially when emotions run high. And if there's one thing I've learned, **nothing stirs up emotions faster than financial stress.**

Money has a way of touching every part of our lives
It's torn marriages apart, created rifts in families, and even dissolved business partnerships.
And more often than not, it's not just the money itself—it's the *different ideologies* around how to handle it that cause the spark.

So in this chapter, let's take a closer look at how Robert (our Performer who sometimes struggles to feel heard) and Tanya navigate emotionally charged financial conversations—and what we can learn from them about the importance of BOUNDARIES in discussions with finances.

The Cost of Silence Isn't Always Financial

Tanya looked over at Robert as he ended yet another tense phone call with his older sister, Layla. Their mother had been diagnosed with early-stage dementia, and the family had been trying to coordinate care, expenses, and schedules. But "trying" was generous.

Robert had been footing most of the bills quietly. Layla had stepped back, claiming her hands were full with her own kids. And the youngest brother, Marcus, hadn't said much of anything. Everyone was doing "something"—but no one was saying what they really felt.

After he hung up, Tanya gently asked, "Are you okay?"

Robert forced a half-smile. "It's fine. It'll work itself out."

But she could tell it wouldn't. Not like that.

Real-Life Tie-In: How Emotions Amplify Financial Conversations

Money isn't neutral. It carries meaning—about love, control, fairness, sacrifice.

61% of Americans say **money is their biggest relationship stressor** *(SunTrust Bank survey). And* In families, it reopens old stories:

- Who was responsible?
- Who was favored?
- Who always had to "step up"?

And in business, money reflects value—but also vulnerability. You start to ask yourself questions:Are they paying me what I'm worth? Are they using me? Am I undervaluing myself just to avoid rocking the boat?

Robert wasn't just avoiding conflict—he was carrying emotional weight silently. And it was bleeding into his relationship with Tanya as well as his work life too. What we experience in our personal lives (good or bad) can impact how we show up professionally. If we are not careful, our burn out can affect our tone and word choice with others.

Business Parallel: Silent Sacrifice Doesn't Scale

I've seen this play out in my own workplace. During a company restructure, I quietly took on extra responsibilities—without asking for more pay. My coworkers praised my dedication. Leadership? They never even acknowledged it.

Everything was affected—my time, my energy, even my bank account. I was spending more, earning the same, and doing it all in the name of being a "good employee" or "team player."

By the time I finally spoke up, I was exhausted, bitter, and one email away from quitting.

That experience taught me something: in business, just because you *can* do more doesn't mean you *should*—especially without a conversation about what you're receiving in return.

58% of employees say they are **uncomfortable discussing compensation** or raises with their employer (Glassdoor).And I realized, I was one of them.

So the next time I was asked to stay late and lead a project, I responded differently:
"It's possible, but can we discuss what that would look like in terms of expectations—and how the team will be contributing?"

No blame. Just boundaries.

A clear signal that while I'm willing to show up, I'm no longer available for silent sacrifice.

Lesson: Silence won't protect you. Boundaries will.

Tactical Communication Analysis: How to Separate Emotions From Financial Discussions (Without Losing Connection)

When it comes to protecting yourself emotionally, that often means protecting yourself financially too.

Boundaries may feel uncomfortable at first, but they're necessary—not to push people away or create tension, but to preserve connection. Clear boundaries help you honor your time, energy, and well-being so you can show up fully and give others the best version of you.

So here are some quick steps you can do to start conversations about money in times where boundaries are being crossed

1. Acknowledge the Emotion—Even If It's Silent

Before numbers, come feelings. Something is making you uncomfortable. Don't ignore it. What is it? Why do you feel this way. Then address it (first with yourself, then with others).

"I've been feeling overwhelmed by everything lately, and I realize I haven't said anything."

Now decide, once again, with yourself first, what do YOU need in order to feel more comfortable in this scenario. Now think of the others, how will this work or not work for them (knowing issues they may have allows you to mentally prepare for it as well as come up with other solutions that don't weigh on you).

Now you can meet with others.

2. Align the Goal

Whether it's with siblings or business partners, start with unity:

"We all want Mom to be okay. Can we talk about what support looks like realistically for each of us?"

IMPORTANT TO NOTE: Once again, before having full conversations on goals with others, it is important to spend time reflecting on what you can commit to as an individual and where YOU are financially. Starting any type of financial conversation with confusion within yourself can be extremely problematic.

3. Keep Emotions Present, But Not in the Driver's Seat

Let emotion inform your empathy—not your decision-making.

It's important to be understanding of where others are coming from, but your needs in any partnership or business decision have to remain at the forefront to come to a proper compromise.

4. Use Clear Language

"I can commit to $300 a month, but I need help making the care plan more sustainable."

"Before we finalize the proposal, I'd like to walk through who's responsible for what.

The Meaningful Rewrite

Now lets take a look at what SHOULD have happened between Robert and Tanya earlier.

After Robert's phone call, Tanya gently asked, "Are you okay?"

Robert paused, the usual "I'm fine" forming on his lips. But this time, he didn't say it.

Instead, he sat down next to her and exhaled deeply. "Honestly? No. I'm not. I feel like I'm carrying all of this alone, and I don't know how to ask them for more without sounding angry or needy."

Tanya nodded, staying quiet just long enough to hold space.

"Have you told them that?" she finally asked.

Robert shook his head. "I thought I could just handle it. That maybe they'd step in if they really wanted to. But... maybe they don't know how I feel. Maybe they think I'm okay with it."

That moment—*that choice to speak*—wasn't a magic fix. But it was the first time Robert let his family in, rather than shutting them out.

Later that week, he sent a group message to his siblings—not demanding, not shaming, but honest. He laid out what had been covered so far, what was coming up next, and what kind of support he needed—financially *and* emotionally.

To his surprise, Layla offered to start covering half of the upcoming home care costs. Marcus didn't say much, but he committed to taking their mother to appointments every other week.

No one became a hero overnight. But the silence was broken.

Because sometimes, the biggest cost isn't what's coming out of your bank account—it's what's being withheld from your heart.

Journal Prompt

Who(or where) in my life am I financially (or emotionally) overextending for without clear agreement?

What fear is keeping me from speaking up—disappointment, judgment, rejection?

What's one sentence I could say to bring clarity to this situation?

Chapter 3

MERGING VISIONS WITHOUT KILLING THE VIBE

When Collaboration Feels More Like Compromise

When Alignment Is Assumed, Not Agreed

Tanya's friend Simone had always been the big-vision type. She could see ten steps ahead of everyone else and had the passion to back it up. Her husband and business partner, Anthony—logical, process-driven, deeply rooted in realism—was her grounding force.

Together, they were launching a wellness brand.

Robert and Tanya had invited them over for dinner, partly to celebrate, partly to decompress. By dessert, Simone's jaw was tight, Anthony was quiet, and Tanya knew *something* was off.

"What's going on?" Tanya asked.

Simone exhaled sharply. "He's trying to turn the brand into a budgeting course. I'm talking soul and storytelling, and he's talking spreadsheets."

Anthony jumped in. "Because people need *structure*—not just feelings. We can't sell vibes."

They weren't disagreeing on the dream—just on the route to get there. And neither had said out loud what they needed from the other. Yet.

Real-Life Tie-In: Collaboration & The Trap of Unspoken Assumptions

Doing business with a loved one is TRICKY, and can be frustrating. I myself have struggled with wanting to keep the love I have for the person, while also being annoyed with them deeply and not wanting to have anything to do with them or the business.

And my attitude surely reflected such thoughts.

Whether it's business, love, or shared leadership—when you merge with someone else's vision, you bring your **unspoken expectations** along with it.

- One person thinks "we're building a lifestyle brand."
- The other thinks "we're building a scalable product."
- One thinks "we'll take it slow."
- The other thinks "let's grind 24/7."

And if those assumptions don't get aired out early, they turn into tension later.

The same shows up in relationships: Robert, for example, often assumes Tanya wants him to be the calm, go-with-the-flow type. Tanya assumes Robert will "step up" when it matters. Neither says what they *actually need* from the other until they're already disappointed.

Tactical Communication Analysis: How to Clarify Expectations Before Resentment Builds

1. Define the Vision—Together

Don't assume alignment. Create it.
Ask:

> "What does success look like—for *you*?"
> "What would make this feel fulfilling for both of us?"

Write it down. Make it visible.

2. Identify Deal-Breakers & Non-Negotiables Early

What can't you compromise on? Time? Boundaries? Profit margins? Values?
Ask:

> "Where are we flexible?"
> "Where are we not?"

This turns future conflicts into *conversations*, not explosions.

3. Assign Roles Based on Strengths—Not Ego

Simone didn't need Anthony to mimic her. She needed him to complement her.
And Anthony didn't need to be the voice of reason—just the voice of *structure.*

Ask:

> "What's your lane?"
> "Where do you want support?"
> "Where do I need to stay out of the way?"

4. Set Emotional Agreements Too

It's not just what you do—it's *how* you do it.
Agree on:

- How you'll handle tension
- How often you'll check in
- What grace looks like when one of you drops the ball

Relationship Tie-In: Even Love Needs a Strategic Plan

From Messy to Meaningful: Rewriting the Moment

The Messy Version

"We should talk about our future sometime," Tanya said casually.
Robert nodded. "Yeah, sure," he mumbled, eyes still on his phone.
The moment passed. The conversation never happened.

Why it's messy:

- Vague language ("sometime")
- No real invitation to engage
- Dismissive or distracted body language
- No timeline, no clarity, no connection

The Meaningful Rewrite

Later that night, Tanya turned to Robert and said,
"We should do that too—define what success looks like for us. Not just in love, but in how we build this life together."
Robert looked at her and said,

"You're right. Can we schedule a check-in next week to talk through what we're building?"
Tanya smiled. That was the most aligned she'd felt in months.

Why this works:

- Specific ask with shared language ("define what success looks like")
- Invitation to collaborate rather than criticize
- Suggests structure and commitment ("schedule a check-in")
- Reinforces emotional safety and connection

Mini-Coaching Moment:

Want alignment? Start with intention.

Avoid vague hints—name what you want, when you want to talk, and why it matters. That's leadership—in relationships *and* in business.

Journal Prompt:

- What expectations have I placed on a partner or collaborator that I never actually communicated?
- What assumptions have I made about their priorities or timelines?
- What would it look like to define shared success—*out loud*?

Part 2

CLEANING UP THE MESS

How We Repair What We've Avoided—Starting With Ourselves

Okay—we've named the mess.

We've unpacked the silence, the assumptions, the conflict avoidance, and the passive "yeses" that cost us clarity.

Now, it's time to clean it up.

Yes, that means having better conversations with the people around us—but more importantly, it means having **honest conversations with ourselves** first. Because messy conversations don't start at the table... they start in our minds, our beliefs, our fears, and our self-talk.

In Part 2, we shift from observation to restoration.

This section is about **repair**—how to restore clarity, confidence, and connection when things have gone off track.

We'll explore how to:

- Reset expectations after miscommunication
- Rebuild trust (with others and yourself)
- Speak from a place of power instead of pain
- And redefine what "speaking up" actually looks like for you

Because the truth is: the *real* messy conversation is often the one we avoid having with ourselves.

Let's clean it up—and make it make sense.

Chapter 4

THE STORIES WE TELL OURSELVES

When Internal Dialogue Becomes the Real Roadblock

Tanya reread the text three times.
Robert had replied: "Sure. If you want to."
That was it. No emoji. No question. Just... flat.

She immediately spiraled:
He's annoyed. He doesn't want to spend time with me. I always push too much. Maybe I shouldn't have asked at all.

By the time they saw each other that night, she was cold, distant, and already convinced she'd done something wrong—based on a story she wrote in her head without any input from him.

Real-Life Tie-In: Inner Dialogue Is the First Conversation

Most of us don't realize that our **first reaction** to a moment isn't based on reality—it's based on the *story* we tell ourselves about it.

We narrate:

- "They're pulling away."
- "They're mad at me."
- "They're probably tired of me."
- "I can't do this"

But those thoughts are **guesses**, not facts. And without checking them, we build emotional walls based on fiction.

People who experience high levels of negative self-talk are 3x more likely to:

- Misinterpret tone
- Avoid direct communication
- Assume others are being critical or disapproving
  (American Psychological Association)

In business and life, I've lost hours—and sometimes opportunities—because I let an internal narrative shape how I showed up externally. You can't communicate clearly if your inner dialogue is cluttered.

Tactical Communication Analysis

How to Interrupt the Internal Spiral

1. Catch the Story in Real-Time

Ask: "What story am I telling myself right now?"
Naming the narrative brings awareness.

In full transparency, my relationship with my own inner thoughts has been the biggest battle I've fought to date. And the inner dialogue I tell myself is always in fact, a fairy tale I am latching on to.

2. Check the Facts

Ask: "What evidence do I *actually* have?"
Is it tone? Timing? A pause? Or your past projecting?

> Most of the time when I slow down and check the evidence, I realize—I don't have much. But here's the truth we don't

like to admit: even **when** I can find "evidence" to support my fear, I still have to ask—*so what?*

Just because something happened before and I didn't like the outcome, doesn't mean it will unfold that way again. And even if it does... haven't I already proven I can survive, recover, and rebuild?

Checking the facts is powerful. But even more powerful is learning to let go of the illusion of control. We don't get to control how other people respond—we only get to choose how we show up and speak our truth.make a decision on how we want to go forward in conversing with the necessary parties.

3. Create a Pause Between Story and Response

Wait before replying. Ask a clarifying question:

> "Hey, your message felt kind of brief—just checking in, is everything okay?"

Clarity is your superpower, but so is emotional detachment from the outcome.

> It's okay to ask. It's okay to get clear. But it's *not* your job to control how the other person responds. Whether the answer is warm, cold, or silent—**you will still be okay**. Your business will be okay. Your relationship can still grow. And *you* will be just as grounded as you decide to be.

Business Tie-In: Reading Into Silence Can Cost You Opportunities

Imagine this:
You pitch a collaboration to a potential partner. They don't respond right away. Then they reply with:

> "Thanks for sending—let me think about it and circle back."

You immediately think: They hated it. I shouldn't have sent it. Maybe I'm not ready for this level.

Now instead of following up, you delay. You doubt. You pull back.

But what if the truth is... they were just in back-to-back meetings? Or unsure of budget? Or genuinely interested, but distracted?

The internal spiral delays momentum. And delayed momentum = missed impact.

We must STOP the messy conversations we are having in our head that could not only delay our progress, but DENY our success in the future.

Still follow the steps giving before:

- Pause before spiraling (Breathe, go touch grass, catch the story you are telling yourself before you spiral)
- Ask: "What do I *know* vs. what am I *assuming*? (i.e. evidence)"
- Follow up confidently:

  "Hey! Just circling back on my last note. Let me know if there are any questions I can answer or ways to make this collaboration easier."

From Messy to Meaningful: Rewriting the Moment

The Messy Version

Tanya sees the flat text and pulls away emotionally.
She sends: "Never mind, forget it."
Robert is confused and withdrawn by the time they connect.

The Meaningful Rewrite

Tanya texts: "Hey, I noticed your message felt kind of quick— so I wanted to check in and make sure everything was ok."

Why this works:

- Clarifies tone without blaming
- Keeps the door open
- Gives Robert space to clarify instead of defend

Journal Prompt:

What story do I tell myself most often in moments of uncertainty?

Where did that script come from?

What would it look like to pause, reframe, and ask instead of assume?

Chapter 5

MAKING ROOM FOR REPAIR

How to Reconnect After Conflict or Distance

Alright y'all... time to get spicy and snatch some edges.

Because no matter which of the three categories you landed in—Overwhelmed & Underheard, The Performer, or The Balanced (ish) One—there's one universal truth:

Everybody and their mama will face conflict.
And guess what? You gotta know how to bounce back from it. That's the real flex of communication—not how cute you sound when things are smooth, but how you speak when stuff hits the fan.

Remember in the last chapter, Tanya did the emotionally mature thing and *gasp* asked Robert if he was okay instead of spiraling into silence? Whew. Growth.

But let's keep it real—what if she didn't?

What if she did what so many of us do after a weird look or dry response? What if she started spiraling, re-reading texts like she's decoding the Dead Sea Scrolls, giving attitude for no reason, or mentally rehearsing an argument that hasn't even happened yet?

And guess what happens next? They get into the argument! You know the one we say we don't want, but then our attitudes always get us into? That one.

Because let's be honest—the messy conversations we have in our heads don't *stay* in our heads.

They sneak out through our side-eyes, our dry "I'm fine"s, and our passive-aggressive plate slamming, or ignoring business emails. Or if you're a really good performer, being pleasant enough to do business with but ice cold in basic human interaction (and didn't we learn we get more bees with honey?)

Or they show up in how we ghost people... or ourselves.
(Hey, that project you've been avoiding because your confidence took a hit? Yeah, that too.)

When that inner mess leaks out? Whew. Chaos.

Bringing our internal mess, to external reality. What do we do to fix things in business and personal AFTER we've allowed internal dialogue to cause a conflict?

Let's see how Tanya and Robert are doing. Buckle up.

—

After their last tense conversation, Robert had gotten quieter. Not angry—just emotionally unavailable.

Tanya didn't know whether to press or pull away.

Finally, she sat beside him and said, "I know I made some assumptions the other day. I want to own that. And I want to get back to us—not avoid each other."

It wasn't about who's right. It was about *who was ready to reconnect.*

Real-Life Tie-In: Repair Starts With Ownership

Okay—full honesty?
This is the chapter where I have to call myself out.
It wasn't until I was deep in my own personal relationship that I realized I **struggle with ownership after conflict**.

We all mess up communication.
We make assumptions. We shut down. We say things the wrong way—or say nothing at all.

But the real secret isn't avoiding the mess.
It's learning how to take accountability and **come back after it.**

90% of people say that when someone takes accountability, they are more likely to forgive and move forward. ***(University of Michigan, Institute for Social Research)***

In relationships *and* in business, people respect you more when you can take responsibility for your part, acknowledge what happened, and re-open the conversation. That's emotional maturity—and it builds trust way faster than pretending nothing happened at all.

Tactical Communication Analysis: The Art of Repair

1. Start with Ownership, Not Blame

"I realized I reacted from a place of frustration, and I want to take accountability."

Let's be real:
Sometimes, when we try to "talk it out," we make it worse. And usually, that's because we're not owning *our* side—we're lowkey still trying to win.

You can't control the other person.
But you **can** own your role in the disconnect.

Even if you don't *feel* sorry, ask:

> "Could my words, tone, or actions have impacted them in a way I didn't intend?"

Accountability isn't about guilt—it's about alignment.
It's about getting on the same page, even if some of the details are still grey.
Just don't walk in defensive. Walk in willing.

2. Clarify the Intention of the Repair

> "I want us to feel connected again, not tense. Can we talk it through?"

After taking accountability, let them know what you *hope* for.

But here's the hard truth: **they may not be ready**.

And that's where maturity comes in—being okay with holding space, not just rushing for relief.

3. Don't Rush the Resolution

Give space for emotional processing. It's not about forcing peace—it's about *inviting it.*

You're not speaking just to be validated—you're speaking to take responsibility and *see* if they're open to reconnection.

Some bridges need time to rebuild. You can't fast-forward someone else's emotions. Which leads to our final point.

4. End with an Invitation, Not a Demand

> "When you're ready, I'd love to reset this conversation."

Business Tie-In: When Leaders Repair the Right Way

Conflict happens at work too—missed deadlines, miscommunication, misunderstood tone in an email or meeting. And just like in personal relationships, *how* you repair determines whether trust is strengthened or slowly eroded.

Here's the trap:

In professional settings, people often pretend the tension never happened. They jump into the next project or send a "per my last email" message and call it closure.

But you know what builds more respect?
Owning your role, even in a small misstep.

In the workplace, when leaders model accountability:

- **85% of employees** feel more **psychologically safe** to admit mistakes and take initiative.
  (Harvard Business Review)

Example:

"Hey, I realize my email yesterday may have come off short. That wasn't my intention. I want us to stay aligned and collaborative—can we reset and move forward together?"

That one moment can shift an entire team culture.

In business, just like in life, *repair builds credibility*. It shows emotional intelligence, leadership, and trustworthiness.

From Messy to Meaningful: Rewriting the Moment

The Messy Version

Robert stays quiet. Tanya avoids it too. Weeks pass. Emotional distance grows. Neither feels safe.

The Meaningful Rewrite

Tanya says: "I've been thinking about our last conversation. I know it got tense, and I allowed myself to take the conversation somewhere it did not have to go. I apologize. I want to repair that if you're open to it."

Why this works:

- Names the conflict gently
- Takes accountability and apologizes
- Expresses care and curiosity
- Creates emotional safety

What conversations have I left “hanging” or unresolved?

What part of that moment do I need to take responsibility for?

What would I say if I gave myself permission to repair, not defend?

Part 3

WINNING THE GAME OF COMMUNICATION

This section closes with how to master communication and create stronger relationships.

How to Master Your Voice and Build Relationships That Work

We've unpacked the mess that can cost us by not speaking up.

You've seen what happens when we DON'T speak up. (Spoiler: chaos, confusion, and emotional hangovers.)
We've cleaned it up—internally and externally by understanding conflict navigation.

Now?

Now it's time to master it.

Not just survive communication—but *own* it.

Part 3 is where we stop playing defense and start playing *to win*. It's time to put things together and to develop a plan to become a Balanced communicator (and if you get off track, how to always find yourself coming back on track).

Because communication isn't just about avoiding conflict—it's about building connection, creating clarity, and showing up with confidence in EVERY space you enter.

This final section is about sharpening your communication game. Because real communication?

It's not just about avoiding awkward convos or keeping the peace.

It's about **building real connection**, **creating clarity**, and **walking into any room with confidence—even when the stakes are high and the group chat is silent.**

Here's what we're about to lock in:

1. How to speak with clarity and conviction (yes, even when your voice is shaking)
2. How to lead hard conversations without losing relationships or your cool
3. How to set boundaries *without* the guilt trip
4. How to build trust, influence, and emotional safety—at home, at work, and everywhere in between (no over-performing required)
5. How to get back on track if you slip into Overwhelmed/Underheard mode again (because grace is part of growth)

You'll pick up the habits and mindset shifts of people who don't just sound good—but actually get results, inspire connection, and leave people saying, "Whew. I needed that."

Because the real win?
Isn't just being heard.
It's being *understood*, *respected*, and *aligned*—especially with the people who matter most.

Let's finish strong. Let's elevate your voice.
And let's make communication your *superpower*.

Chapter 6

THE POWER OF SPEAKING UP (EVEN WHEN YOU WANT TO RUN AWAY)

How Setting Boundaries Creates Safety, Not Separation

Robert and Tanya were getting ready for a weekend visit to his family's house. Tanya hesitated as she zipped her bag.
"You told your mom we're not staying overnight?" she asked.

Robert's family was known for not having boundaries. They'll walk in any room they want when they want, stay up loudly all hours of the night, and ask any question that comes to mind.

While well intentioned people, Tanya had enough of her fill the past 5 years. They had both already agreed to stay in a hotel to give them (mainly Tanya) time to recharge.

Robert winced. "I figured we could just play it by ear."

Tanya froze. This is what she feared. Robert had a habit of not wanting to upset his family (primarily his mother). He always prefers to suffer in silence than actually say what's on his mind with anyone, but least of all his mother.

"Robert—we *talked* about this. I need us to have boundaries around time with your family. It's not about being rude—it's about preserving my peace."

"I just didn't want to make a thing out of it," he said.

"Well, it already *is* a thing. Because now I feel like you chose convenience over my comfort," she replied, holding back tears.
"For once, I need you to have my back."

She didn't yell. She didn't storm off. But she didn't back down either.

Why Setting Boundaries Feels Scary (But Is Necessary)

Speaking up for yourself—especially with the people you love—can feel like betrayal.
You think: *What if I upset them? What if they take it the wrong way? What if I lose the relationship entirely?*

But here's the truth: **if you constantly abandon your needs to maintain peace, you're building resentment instead of real connection.**

Setting boundaries doesn't push people away. It **invites people to meet you in truth.**

And listen—I've run from so many conversations where I should've stood firm (my therapist and closest friends can attest to that).I've said yes when my gut was screaming no. And every time, it cost me more energy than just saying what I needed in the first place.

The worst part, isn't just that I take away my own peace, but I also ensure that the other people didn't have a chance to show up for me or to grow with me. I handicapped the relationship.

Business Tie-In – Boundaries in the Workplace

Setting boundaries isn't just a personal skill—it's a **professional survival tool.**
In business, blurred lines lead to burnout.

76% of employees report experiencing burnout **at least sometimes**, and those who set clear boundaries are **half as likely** to report feeling chronically overwhelmed.*(Gallup, 2023)*

Whether it's a client asking for last-minute changes *outside the scope*, or a colleague constantly pushing past your time or priorities, the fear of being "difficult" keeps many people saying *yes* when they really mean *no*.

But here's the truth:
Clear boundaries signal self-respect—and teach others how to respect your time and talent.

Example

You're a consultant, and a client emails you with a "quick" task on a weekend.

The spiral sounds like:

> "I should just do it so I don't lose the relationship."

But the leadership response sounds like:

> "Thanks for reaching out! I can prioritize that first thing Monday morning. If it's urgent, I'm happy to provide an additional invoice for weekend support."

That's not rude—it's respectful. And it protects your long game.

Boundary-setting in business protects your peace, your brand, and your energy.

Tactical Communication Analysis: How to Stand Firm Without Guilt

1. Start With Clarity, Not Apology

> We don't apologize for boundaries.

> "I've decided I won't be staying overnight. I need to honor what's best for my energy."

Don't lead with "I'm sorry"—lead with self-respect. You are NOT sorry and have done nothing wrong. You are just communicating and letting them know what you are thinking.

2. Anchor It in Values

> "Spending time with your family matters to me, *and* so does coming home to rest."

This shows it's not either/or—it's both/and. This also ensures that you are showing the other person that you do understand their own desires, while still establishing your needs/values. This opens the door for conversations on what compromise could be (or a new idea that works for both your values all together).

3. Repeat Calmly If Needed

> "I've already communicated my boundary. I won't be changing it."

You don't have to argue. You don't have to justify it endlessly. State it. Stick with it. And do it without guilt. Be open if need be to other solutions, but those solutions should still accommodate what you have stated as a value/need.

4. Expect Discomfort, Not Disconnection

People may feel surprised or even disappointed. That doesn't mean you've done something wrong.

Discomfort is part of growth—for them *and* for you.

The truth is, we're not afraid of the boundary, we're afraid of the reaction. But we can't be so afraid of losing those we love (or the contract/client we want badly), that we lose ourselves.

The moment you are willing to compromise yourself to the point that you disrespect your own boundaries or value, you have already lost.

In business and in personal, be willing to disagree. And if a compromise cannot be reached because the other person is unwilling to help come up with one, sit in knowing that you did everything you could on your end.

From Messy to Meaningful: Rewriting the Moment

The Messy Version

Robert avoids telling his family about the boundary. Tanya stays overnight, resentful. The next morning, she's distant and emotionally shut down.

The Meaningful Rewrite

Tanya says: "I really need us to be on the same page about this boundary. It's important to me that you communicate it with your family. I'll go with you   but only if we're leaving at the time we agreed."

Why this works:

- Clear request
- Shared accountability
- Reasserts partnership, not just personal preference

Journal Prompt:

Where have I said "yes" to keep the peace, when I really wanted to say "no"?

What boundary do I need to hold—without apology?

How can I prepare to stand firm, even if it's uncomfortable?

Chapter 7

THE LANGUAGE OF LEADERSHIP (IN LOVE & BUSINESS)

How Clear Communication Builds Strong Teams and Stronger Trust

Lets check back in with Simone and Anthony, friends to Tanya and Robert. When we last saw them, they were struggling to establish who leads what, the vision of their company, and how to really work together as a team who also happen to be husband and wife.

Both have been doing the work to be better communicators with each other by being clients of La'Shondra Johnson and reading her book "Messy Conversations" (have you heard of this amazing woman?)

But doing the work isn't just on fixing the past, it's on navigating the present better. Let's see how they're doing.

Anthony was exhausted.

Their brand launch was two weeks away, and he felt like she was carrying the weight of it all.
Simone had been helping, sure—but she hadn't been leading.

"I'm feeling drained and I need you to take more initiative," Anthony finally said during a late-night planning session.
"It's feeling like you are waiting for me to direct everything, and I'm not saying you are doing this intentionally, but noting what I am observing. I

don't need a follower—I need a partner. Can we talk about how we can share the responsibility a bit more?"

Simone paused. She could've gotten defensive.
Instead, she said, "You're right. I've been afraid of stepping on your toes, but in the process, I've stopped showing up as a leader."

That conversation? Changed everything.

Real-Life Tie-In: Leadership Grows from Ownership

Whether you're leading a team, a household, or a relationship—**leadership starts with communication**.

And communication isn't just about talking—it's about listening, anticipating, following through, and *owning your presence* in every room you walk into.

In love and business, you can't lead if you're hiding.
And you can't inspire if you're waiting to be told what to do.

Leadership grows the moment you stop managing impressions and start standing in your impact.

Rather than let himself grow into being burned out and resentful, Anthony spoke up about how he was feeling. And rather than getting defensive, Simone took a second to listen to what he said and process it so that she can take ownership on her end. And this? This is what I call GROWTH!

Business Tie-In – Leadership Is a Communication Skillset

Leadership isn't about titles—it's about *how you show up when clarity, accountability, and vision are needed.*

In business, most teams fail not because of bad people—but because of **unclear communication and unmet expectations**.

Companies with strong internal communication are **50% more likely to reduce employee turnover** (Brosix,2024)

Whether you're leading a team or collaborating with peers, your **language creates culture**.

Example

Imagine a team meeting where deadlines have been missed repeatedly. A passive leader says nothing. A controlling leader blames everyone. But a communication-forward leader says:

> "We've missed a few marks lately, and I think part of that is on how we've communicated expectations. Let's clarify timelines and build a better check-in system together."

That's real leadership.
It builds buy-in instead of resentment.
It creates clarity instead of confusion.
And it invites accountability—without shame.

Your words either build alignment or create distance. Choose them with care.

Tactical Communication Analysis: How to Lead With Language That Builds Trust

1. Lead With Alignment

> "Here's what I see as our shared goal. Let's get clear on how we get there together."

When people know what they're working toward, they lead with you—not behind you.

2. Name the Gap Without Shame

> "I've noticed we're falling behind on updates. How can we close that gap together?"

Call out what's not working, *without* assigning blame.Once we get out of our own heads about being right, the focus can just be on getting to our end goal *together*.

3. Model Vulnerability

> "I'm learning to lead better, and I want your honest feedback too."

Leadership isn't being perfect. It's creating space for progress.

4. Close With Confidence

> "Let's decide next steps before we leave this conversation."

Confidence isn't control—it's clarity. Great leaders don't just inspire; they organize the action.

From Messy to Meaningful: Rewriting the Moment

The Messy Version

Anthony keeps pushing through alone. Simone stays quiet. Resentment builds, and their launch suffers because the team isn't aligned.

The Meaningful Rewrite

Anthony says: "I need your leadership. I feel like I've been directing everything, and I'm burned out."
Simone replies: "Thanks for saying that. I've been uncertain about my role, but I'm ready to step up—let's reset."

Why this works:

- Invites clarity
- Reduces power struggle
- Builds shared ownership

Journal Prompt:

Where in my life or business have I avoided leading out of fear of conflict or overstepping?

What would leading with clarity—and not control—look like for me?

How can I invite shared ownership in my relationships or team?

Chapter 8

SPEAK IT. MEAN IT. KEEP GOING.

How to Stay Aligned With Your Voice in Every Room You Enter

Our main character, and also a recent client of La'Shondra Johnson, Robert, often struggled with being overwhelmed and underheard in every area of his life. But he has been doing the internal work necessary to speak up more in his family, and it is also starting to take shape in his business life.

He is taking more initiative, while still nervous, he is excited to see how good life can get when he bets on himself.

Let's see where speaking with confidence gets him.

Robert stood outside the conference room, adjusting his blazer. He was about to pitch his team's strategy to the executive board—a room he'd once avoided out of fear of being seen, heard, or challenged.

Tanya had texted him that morning:

> "You already have the power. Just speak like you know it."

This time, he didn't shrink.
He led with clarity, paused with purpose, and challenged assumptions with confidence—not ego.
And when the CEO asked him to tweak a section of the proposal, Robert said:

> "That's a fair ask. But here's why I believe our original direction aligns more with the company's long-term goal."

No people-pleasing. No fake yes. Just a powerful, grounded voice.
When the meeting ended, one of the VPs said, "That's the first time someone's made that kind of challenge—and backed it up with that much grace."

Robert didn't just communicate. He led.

Real-Life Tie-In: Your Voice is Your Power—Even in Uncertainty

Growth will test your communication.

You'll be celebrated one day and questioned the next. You'll be asked to lead, to pause, to speak up when it's easier to stay quiet.

And the question becomes:
Can you stay grounded in your voice—through success, through discomfort, through shifting expectations?

Because communication mastery isn't about always being the loudest or the most polished.
It's about knowing who you are, what you stand for, and staying consistent—even when the pressure is on.

There's a classic song by New Edition called *Can You Stand the Rain?*
It's usually about romantic relationships, but I like to flip the lens:

Can you stand the rain when the storm is *internal*?
When growth feels uncomfortable?
When your boundaries get tested?
When the spotlight comes with a little shade?

Can you *still* show up in your truth when everything around you is shifting—when you have to choose between pleasing others or honoring yourself?

Can you quiet the downpour of self-doubt long enough to hear your own voice?

If you even *thought* about saying no, let me just remind you:
This was a rhetorical question.
You *absolutely* can and will stand the rain.
Because pressure makes diamonds.
And scared money don't make money.

Tactical Communication Analysis: How to Keep Showing Up With Confidence

1. Build Your Communication Rituals

Whether it's journaling before big conversations, reviewing your values, or rehearsing key points aloud—build routines that **reconnect you to your voice**.

> Confidence is built in preparation—not pressure.

2. Speak in Alignment, Not Performance

Drop the performance persona.
People are moved by *clarity, not perfection.*

> "Here's what I believe. Here's why. And I'm open to conversation—not just compliance."
>
> This also means that you are coming into conversations well informed on the topics, the people you are speaking to and anything else you know you need. A well informed person, is a confident person.

3. Pause Before Pivoting

When things shift, don't scramble. Pause, reflect, then respond.

> "Let me take a moment to consider that before I reply." That one sentence protects your peace *and* your professionalism. The art of the pause is just another note to take your time. Do not rush. I love a good pause after I say something heavy (or I call it "meaty"). It's a great way to give people time to think or realize the weight of what you have said, and also gives you time to consider what else you need to say.

4. Protect Your Voice from Burnout

Your voice is a resource. Protect it from environments that ask for too much and offer too little. Say no. Take breaks. Replenish.

> A burned-out communicator can't connect. Build in your own recovery time.

Business Tie-In: The Voice That Carries is the One That's Consistent

In leadership, branding, and sales—people trust **what feels steady**.

You don't need to be flashy. You don't need to know all the answers. But you *do* need to sound like someone who's done the work to know what they stand for.

Your business voice is built one conversation at a time:

- The clarity in how you pitch (A elementary student should be able to understand what you are talking about in 3 sentences or less)
- The confidence in how you follow up

- The calm in how you navigate conflict
- The care in how you listen and respond

Leaders who win long-term are those who **stay in alignment**, even when things shift.

From Messy to Meaningful: Rewriting the Moment

The Messy Version

Robert gets challenged during the board meeting and quickly folds, saying: "Sure, whatever works."
He leaves feeling small and dismissed.

The Meaningful Rewrite

He says: "That's helpful insight. I still believe our direction works best for the company goals—but I'm open to refining it together."

Why this works:

- Anchors in shared goals
- Stays assertive without ego
- Shows flexibility without self-erasure

Journal Prompt:

What is one conversation coming up where I need to show up more fully?

What support or prep would help me feel aligned in that moment?

What belief about my voice do I need to retire—and what truth do I need to replace it with?

Chapter 9

THE SHIFT

Let's get one thing straight: just because you've been working on your communication game—and you're seeing real wins—doesn't mean you'll nail it every time. Growth doesn't come with a perfection clause.

Every skill, especially new ones, needs reps. It's like the gym... but for your mouth.

And as the iconic philosopher Aaliyah once said:
"If at first you don't succeed, dust yourself off and try again."

So give yourself grace.
Refocus.
And get back to being that *balanced communicator* you already know how to be.

When Silence Was Louder

Robert stood at the sink, rinsing the last of the dishes, the sound of running water the only thing filling the space between him and Tanya . She stood across from him, arms crossed, eyes scanning the floor like she was waiting for the right words to appear there.

"You shut down every time I try to tell you how I feel," she said finally, her voice soft but firm. "And I get it—you're tired, you're stretched. But silence isn't safer. It's just heavier."

He dried his hands, careful, like the towel in his grasp might tear. "I didn't know how to respond without making it worse."

Tanya shrugged. "Doing nothing made it worse."

The conversation didn't end with a hug. There were no dramatic exits. Just two people standing in the quiet space between hurt and healing, finally acknowledging that pretending wasn't working.

Robert felt guilty. He had been doing so much better,and now here he was avoiding conversations.Again. ***Even balanced communicators can lose their footing.***

The key is knowing how to get it back.

Real-Life Tie-In: When Avoidance Replaces Honesty and recovery is the skill.

Let's be real: You can *know* all the tools, lead the workshops, even *coach other people* through their tough conversations (whew that last one felt personal for a second)—and still find yourself slipping into old patterns when emotions hit. That doesn't make you a fraud. It makes you human.

We've all been Robert or Tanya. We've avoided a hard conversation, assuming that silence would hurt less than honesty. In business, the same pattern repeats—misalignment festers when feedback isn't shared. In relationships, assumptions widen the gap when clarity is missing.

Unspoken expectations are like invisible contracts—binding, but never agreed upon.

We tell ourselves, "If I just stay quiet, it'll pass." But emotions don't expire—they echo until they're expressed.

The longer you wait to speak your truth, the harder it becomes to find your voice when it matters most.

But here's the difference between a messy communicator and a balanced one:

A balanced communicator doesn't pretend the misstep didn't happen. They correct it.

Your Comeback Blueprint: How to Return to Balance After a Slip

When you find yourself off-track, here's how to realign:

1. **Name It Without Shame:**
   "I realized I shut down instead of speaking up. That wasn't fair to you or helpful to the conversation."

2. **Reconnect to the Message:**
   Get back to *why* you wanted to communicate in the first place. Hint: It's not to win—it's to connect, clarify, or grow.

3. **Rebuild in Real Time:**
   Use language that brings you back into dialogue, not defense.
   Try: "Can we try again?" or "Let me explain that better."

4. **Learn, Don't Linger:**
   The goal isn't to wallow. It's to catch the pattern *sooner* next time and shift. That's growth.

Business Tie-In: Silence Costs More Than Speaking Up

In teams and partnerships, silence shows up as:

- Avoiding conflict rather than resolving it
- Withholding feedback to "protect" feelings
- Assuming alignment instead of confirming it

Collaboration thrives on clarity. Even the tough conversations.

The most effective teams and leaders don't avoid tension—they manage it with honesty, humility, and care.

So whether it's your co-founder, client, or colleague—say what needs to be said before silence becomes resentment.

And if for whatever reason, you slipped. Immediately begin to take ownership and start the necessary conversations.

Whether it's a botched client convo, a passive-aggressive email you wish you'd unsent, or a team meeting where you *definitely* let your silence say too much—it's not the end. It's a detour.

Here's your recovery script:

> "I realized I didn't bring my full self to that conversation. That's on me. I want to revisit it because I care about the outcome *and* the relationship."

That one sentence? Professional gold.

From Messy to Meaningful: Rewriting the Moment

The Messy Version:

Tasha says, "You shut down every time," and Robert deflects with, "I don't want to fight." The conversation ends in cold silence.

The Meaningful Rewrite:

Robert replies, "You're right—I've been shutting down. Not because I don't care, but because I didn't know how to respond. Can we try again, slower this time?"

Why this works:

- Names the issue without blame
- Expresses care without performance
- Invites connection, not closure

Final Thought: Silence is Only Golden in Meditation–Not in Miscommunication

You will slip. That's not failure—it's feedback.

The real flex is being able to catch yourself and come back with honesty, humility, and alignment.

You already have the tools. Now, when things go left, you know how to gently guide them back right.

Take a deep breath. Reset. Speak again.

Because silence may protect your ego—but communication protects the relationship.

Reclaim the Unsaid

Take a moment to revisit a time you avoided communication out of fear.

- Who was involved?
- What was left unsaid?
- What did you assume about the other person?
- What part of your truth did you silence?
- If you could rewrite that moment, what would you say now?

Use this as a low-pressure space to express what's been sitting in your chest. You don't have to send it—but you do need to face it.

____

____

____

Because avoidance may protect your ego, but it often starves your growth.

____

____

____

And this chapter—the one you're living—is worth writing with boldness.

____

____

____

Chapter 10
WHAT NOW

WE DID IT! We made it to balanced communicator status! *Wipes forehead dramatically like we just ran a marathon and a TED Talk at the same time.*

I know what you're thinking:
"Okay, I've done the work... it only gets easier from here, right?"
WRONG.

Here's the thing:
Speaking your truth.
Setting boundaries.

Navigating financial matters in personal and business.

Knowing how to speak up for yourself and your brand to potential partners or clients.
Being the person willing to talk it out—even when no one else wants to?

That's not the norm.
In fact, about 1 in 3 adults report anxiety around *all* of the above.

But here's the good news:
The more you practice, the more peace you'll feel.
You'll be so grounded in who you are, so proud of the person you're becoming, that the discomfort?
Totally worth it.

Higher emotional intelligence resulting from communication development leads to better **conflict resolution, decision-making**, and **workplace well-being** **(Very Well Minded)**

How else do I know this is worth it?

Because I've lived it.
And truthfully? I'm still living it—*daily.*
This isn't about perfection. It's about persistence.
And now that you've got the tools, the awareness, and the receipts to prove you've done the work...

Let's talk about what to do next.

The Day After the Truth

Tanya stared at her phone.
Still no response.

Not from her old boss Chris.
Not from the job she risked everything to pitch to.
Not from the best friend she finally confronted.

She wasn't surprised. But that didn't mean it didn't sting.

The silence after the truth can be louder than the lie ever was.

She slid her phone under a pillow and whispered, "God, please tell me I didn't just blow up my life for nothing."

But somewhere beneath her fear, there was something else.
Relief.

The weight of pretending had lifted. The stories she told to keep the peace? Released.

This was the cost of alignment: discomfort, grief, and the strange freedom of knowing you didn't abandon yourself—even when others may have.

Real-Life Tie-In: Clarity Costs, But Confusion Costs More

It's tempting to think that doing the right thing will feel good immediately.

But the truth is, sometimes the right thing feels lonely before it feels liberating.

Especially when you've spent years performing peace, avoiding conflict, or downplaying your truth to make others comfortable.

The "after" is quiet.
But it's in that quiet that you begin to rebuild.

Not around who left, but around what stayed:
Your integrity.
Your voice.
Your self-trust.

What's meant for you—the paid speaking gigs, the dream clients, the juicy corporate contracts—won't be scared off by your boundaries.
In fact, they'll be drawn to your confidence, your clarity, and the way you own your value without flinching.

Because aligned opportunities don't need you to shrink—they need you to *shine.*

Communication Analysis: The Courage to Continue

When you've just made a bold move in communication—spoken up, walked away, owned your truth—the aftermath is full of emotional noise:

- Doubt: "Was I too much?"

- Guilt: "Should I have softened it?"
- Fear: "What if they never come back?"

But this is where emotional maturity deepens.
It's not just about saying the thing—it's about holding yourself steady after you've said it.

It's about:

- Trusting that clarity was worth it
- Reframing solitude as peace, not punishment
- Being proud of who you were in the moment truth was needed most

Business Tie-In: Leadership in the Aftermath

In business, leaders face this question all the time: "What now?"

After delivering tough feedback.
After terminating a contract.
After pivoting the mission.

After telling someone "No" to their business idea or proposition.

Strong communication isn't only measured in how you deliver—it's measured in how you recover.

- Did you follow up?
- Did you make space for processing?
- Did you stand by your values while staying open to growth?

People remember how you communicate *after* the climax. That's what defines your culture. Remember, we want to sustain relationships, even after discomfort. Just because we are not working together on a project anymore, does not mean a bridge has to be burned. If a relationship can be sustained for future endeavors (or at the very least for a good reputation) then always do so.

Holding Yourself in the Quiet

Think about a moment where you finally said the hard thing—or wish you had.

- What happened afterward?
- What emotions came up in the silence?
- What did you learn about yourself in that space?
- What's one way you can affirm your own growth right now?

Your voice matters.
Your growth matters.
And even in the quiet, you are becoming someone worth listening to.

The question isn't just, "What now?"

____

____

____

____

It's, "Who am I now that I've told the truth?"

____

____

____

____

Bonus—Chapter 11

WRITE YOUR OWN ENDING

By now, you've met people who love deeply but don't always communicate clearly. People who apologize with flowers instead of words. People who push others away when what they really want is to be pulled closer. People who struggle to speak up for themselves in business. People who are trying—desperately—to get it right, even when they don't have the tools (and by now you should know which one of these you are).

Maybe you saw a version of yourself in Tanya, always questioning if she's too much.
Maybe you felt a lump in your throat reading Robert's silence, the way he wanted peace but never said what he needed.
Maybe you've been the sister, the business partner, the friend who said "I'm fine" when you weren't.

This book wasn't meant to give you neat solutions or perfect scripts.
It was written to spark something—*awareness.*
Because when you can see the pattern, you can disrupt it. And when you can disrupt it, you can finally choose differently.

The Truth About Communication and Conflict

Let's keep it real:
People aren't mind readers.
Avoidance is not peace.

And passive-aggressive silence is still communication—it just says, "You're not worth the effort of clarity."

Relationships—whether romantic, family, or professional—aren't ruined by conflict.
They're ruined by how we respond to it. Or more often... how we don't.

So here's what I'll leave you with:

Let This Be the Start of Something New

Grab a notebook or open your Notes app. Take inventory. Ask yourself:

- Who do I need to have an honest conversation with?
- What role do I play in the patterns I complain about?
- Where have I been showing up out of fear instead of love?
- What does emotional safety/boundaries *actually* look like for me—and am I creating it for others?In business?In my personal life?

Start with one person. One moment. One truth.One business scenario. You don't need to fix every situation overnight. You just need to show up differently in one of them—and let that ripple.

A Few Tools to Carry Forward

Here's a short list of strategies you can return to anytime when communicating in difficult times:

- **The Pause Practice**: Before reacting, take a deep breath and ask, "What am I actually feeling right now?"
- **Repair Over Ruin**: When something breaks, choose to *repair* the connection, not punish the person.
- **Check Your Filters**: Ask yourself, "Am I hearing this through pain or through presence?"

- **The Love + Logic Framework**: Communicate what you feel (love), and what you need (logic).
- **Own Your Story**: Speak from "I," not "You." It disarms defensiveness and brings clarity.

You're Not Alone in This Work (And You're Not Crazy, Either)

Let's be real—becoming a balanced communicator isn't a one-and-done. It's a *practice*. A muscle. A journey. And spoiler alert: growth is *not* linear.

Some days it's quiet and calm. Other days it's messy, awkward, or downright uncomfortable.
Sometimes you'll revisit the same trigger 42 times like, "Wait... I *thought* I healed this already?"
(Been there. Cried there. Grew there.)

But guess what?
You are not alone.

Every character in this book—yes, even the ones who fumbled—is proof that transformation is possible.
Even when it's inconvenient.
Even when it hurts.
Even when you're *this close* to choosing silence instead of speaking up.

So as you turn this final page, I want to leave you with two things:

The Truth:

You have more power than you think.
You can't control how others respond—but you *can* control how you show up, how you communicate, and what you allow.

The Invitation:

Use that power to create a life that actually fits.
The kind of love, leadership, connection, and confidence that feels like *you*—the you who doesn't shrink, avoid, or explode, but communicates with intention, courage, and grace.

You're not here to be perfect.
You're here to be present.
To practice.
To *get back up* after the messy moments.
And most importantly—to show up for conversations that matter.

So go on—use what you've learned.
Speak up.
Set the boundary.
Ask the hard question.
Apologize.
Clarify.
Reset.
Repeat.

And whatever you do...

Don't mess this up.
(Not because you can't make mistakes—but because now? You know better.
And knowing better means communicating better.
One honest, messy, brave conversation at a time.)
I'm rooting for your voice.

—La'Shondra

EVERYDAY EXERCISES TO TAKE YOU FROM BEING OVERWHELMED TO A BALANCED COMMUNICATOR

Communication *is* your leadership style.

Whether you're leading a team, pitching a project, or navigating a tough talk with a client or co-founder—people remember how you made them feel. The best leaders don't avoid tension, they manage it with care.
The best communicators don't perform, they connect.

So here's your real-world communication glow-up plan:

1. The Mirror Moment (Self-Awareness Check-In)

Set a 5-minute timer and jot down:

- When conflict about ____ happens, I usually: ______________ (use this to think of multiple scenarios in business and personal life)
- I feel most triggered when: ______________________
- A childhood moment that shaped how I communicate in positive/negative way: ___________
- One pattern I want to break or upgrade: ___________ (and give yourself a deadline or mini goals to reach as you work on this to ensure that you aren't just saying it, but practicing it too)

This is your personal communication blueprint. Use it like a GPS.

2. The "Hard Conversation" Script

For personal *or* business use (yes, even that co-worker who sends confusing emails at 11 p.m.):

> "Hey, I've been thinking about something I want to talk through. I value our relationship and want us to flow better. What I'm feeling is __________. What I need is __________. I'd love to hear your side too."

No passive-aggression. No dragging. Just clarity with kindness. Feel free to of course edit the word choice to match how you speak.

3. The Trigger Translator

Before you snap, ask:

- What story am I telling myself right now?
- Am I reacting to *this* or to something old that just resurfaced?

Bosses, speakers, partners—this works in *every* room you enter.

4. The 24-Hour Rule

Before you clap back, step back.
If you're heated, pause. Give it a day.
Show up with a solution, not just emotion. In other words, process what you are feeling, why that might be, and what needs to happen going forward for this to work out better in the future.

5. The "What I Wish They Knew" Letter

No, you don't have to send it. But write it. It's healing. It's grounding. Great leaders reflect before they react. Get the feelings out. And then, if you feel it's necessary go back to exercise two and prepare to have the conversation with this person.

6. Create a "Safe Space" Signal

For relationships *and* team dynamics:

- A phrase like "Can we pause and reset?"
- A gesture or code word (yes, even in meetings!)
  Normalize creating safety in tough convos.

7. Schedule Communication Check-Ins

Whether it's your boo or your board:

- What's working?
- What's feeling off?
- How can we support each other better?

Growth doesn't require a breakdown. Just a check-in.

8. Add Grace to the Grind

You're not a robot. Neither are they.
Growth is messy—but progress is still progress.

Say it with me:

> "I can grow and still get it wrong sometimes. That doesn't cancel the progress I've made."

Your Final Challenge

Pick one of these tools and use it this week.
Then come back to it.
Track how you felt *before* and *after.*
Watch what shifts when you communicate with intention instead of assumption.

This is how we stop messing it up—
not by being perfect.
But by being **present**.

So go ahead.
Rewrite your ending.
Make it honest.
Make it powerful.
Makc it profitable.
But most of all—
Make it yours.

Let's go get your voice paid, protected, and in position to *make the impact you desire, while building the revenue you deserve.*